BUILDING A BODY

Anatomy and Physiology

All Rights reserved. No part of this book may be reproduced or used in any way or form or by any means whether electronic or mechanical, this means that you cannot record or photocopy any material ideas or tips that are provided in this book.

Copyright 2016

All about the amazing machine...

Let's explore your anatomy.

The human body makes you and me. It is the structure that is made up of a head, a neck, a trunk, arms and hands as well as legs and feet. But your body hosts so much more.

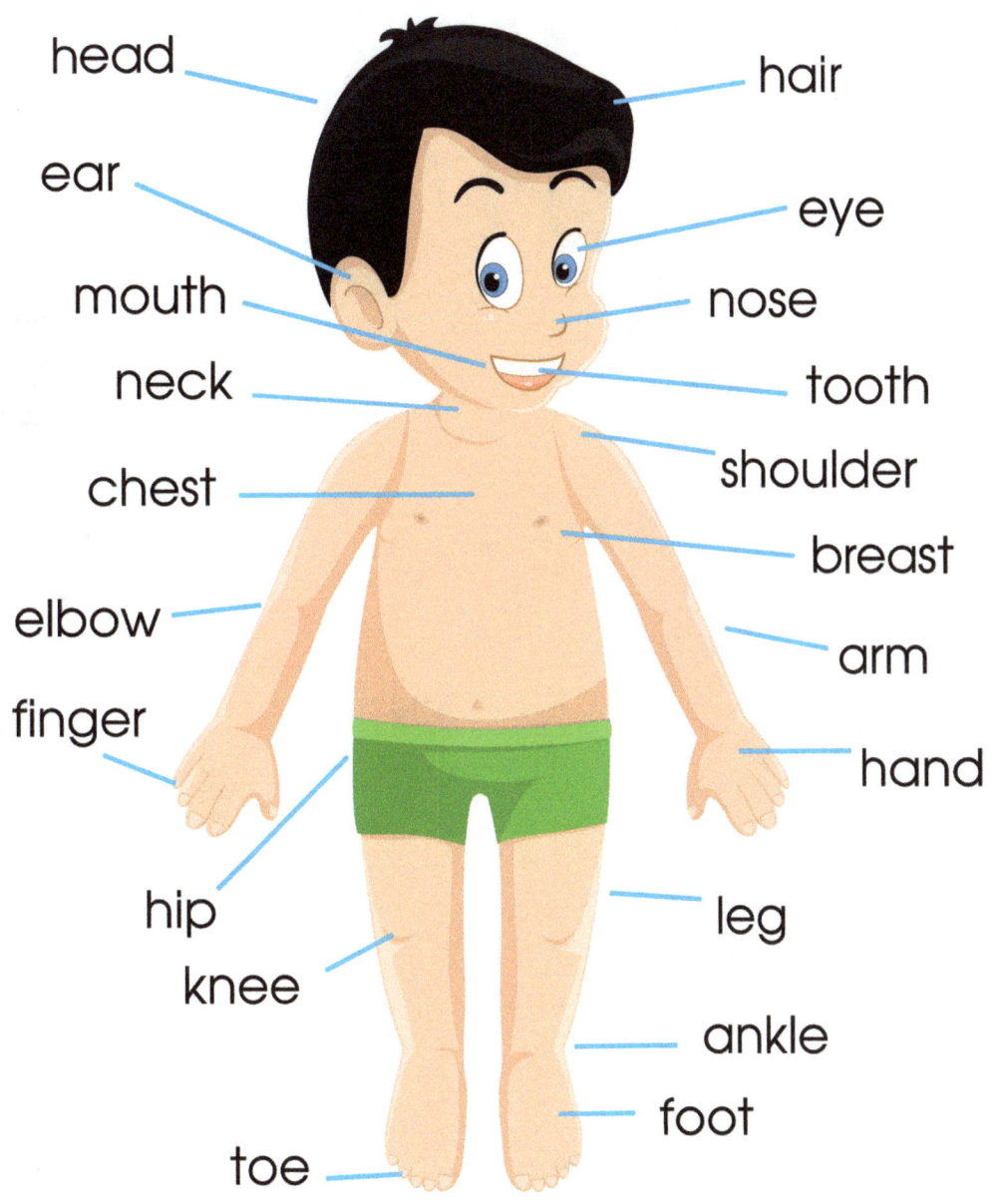

My Body

WHAT IS HUMAN ANATOMY?

It is the study of the systems of the human body to explain how the structures and organs of the body work. The body is made up of cells, tissues and organs. All the body parts function in a coordinated manner.

NERVOUS SYSTEM

All the body senses are controlled by the Nervous System. Its largest organ is the brain.

NERVOUS SYSTEM

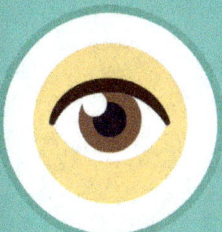

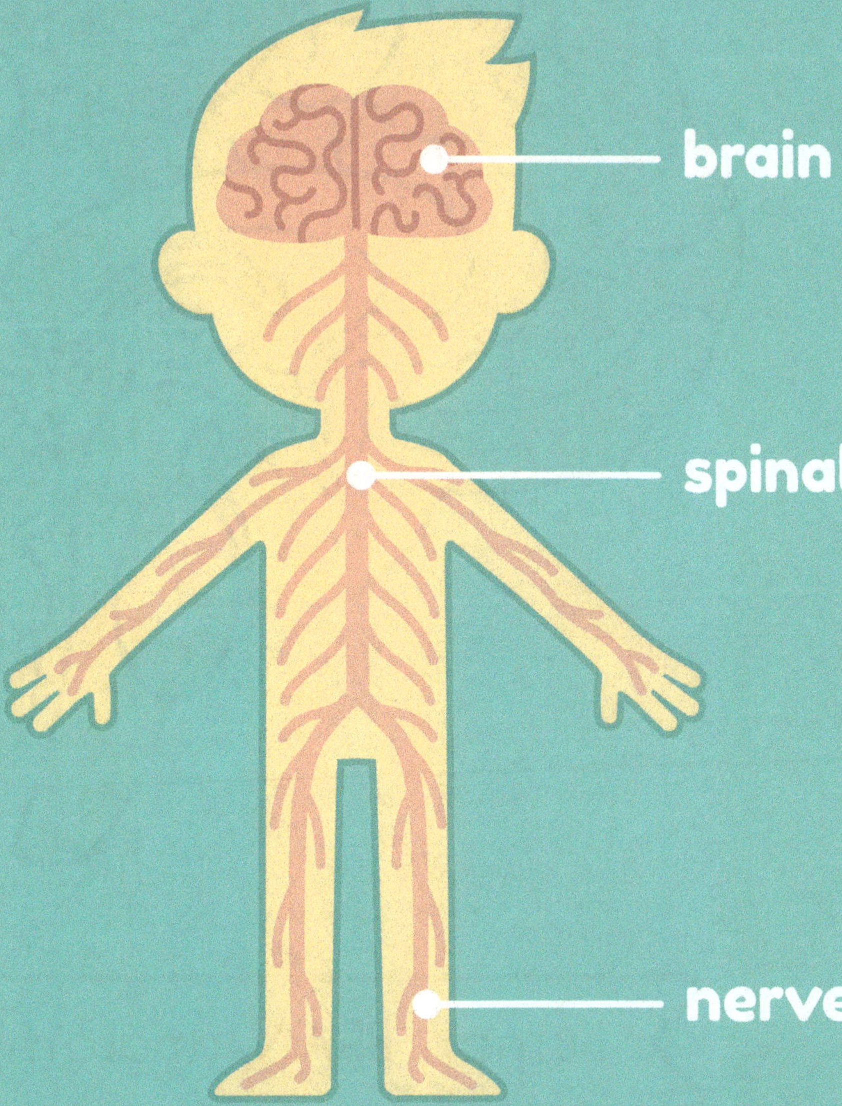

- brain
- spinal cord
- nerves

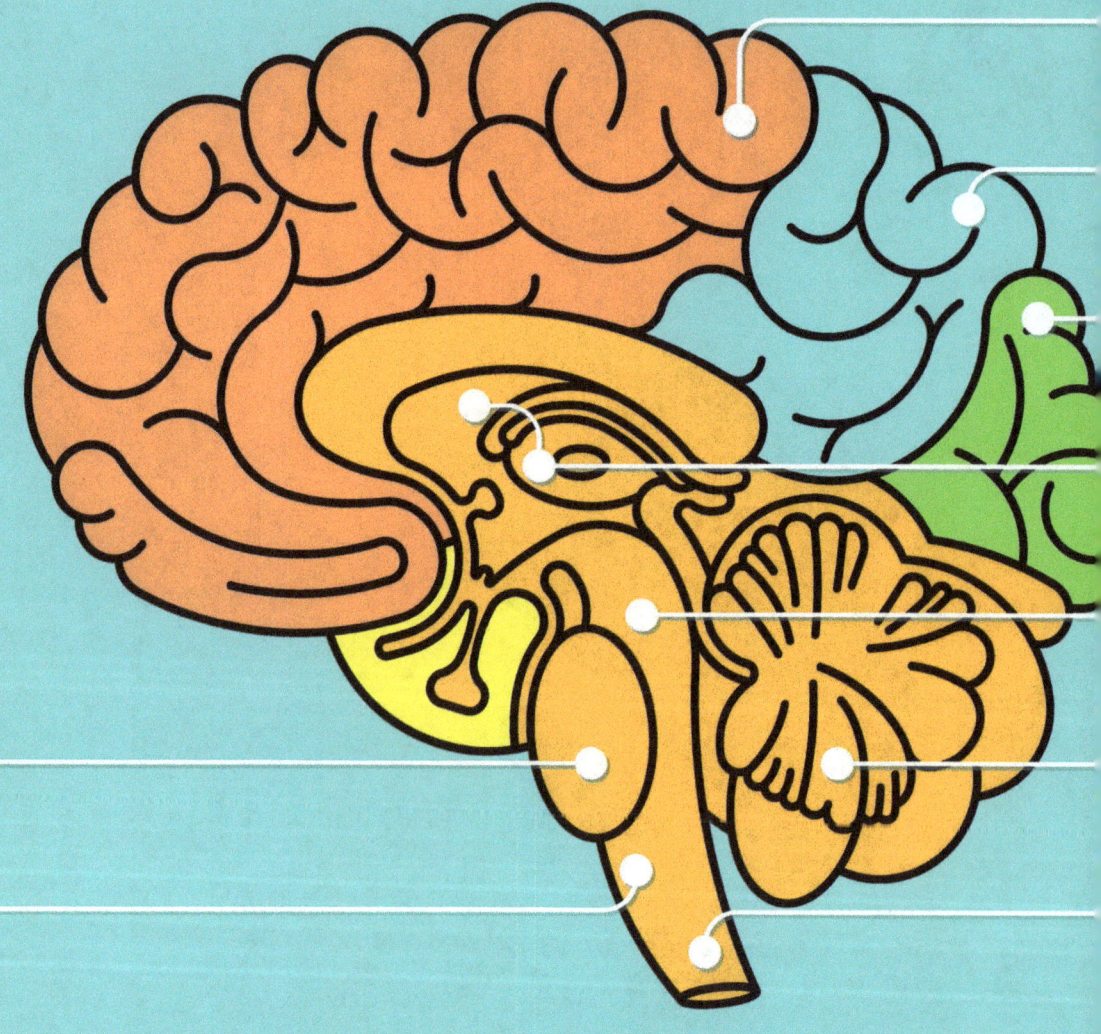

- frontal lobe
- parietal lobe
- occipital lobe
- diencephalon
- midbrain
- cerebellum
- spinal cord

THE HUMAN BRAIN

It is considered as the most complex and the most detailed of all the body parts. It is the computer of our body.

The functions of other body parts are dependent on the brain. It is responsible for sending signals or tiny electrical impulses to the nerves.

Then, the nerves help decide when and how our body moves. The brain is protected by the skull and is floating in the cerebrospinal fluid.

THE CIRCULATORY SYSTEM

It is responsible for delivering nutrients to the other organs of the body. It also carries oxygen and water to the different cells in the body. The wastes that cells create are removed by the circulatory system so it keeps the body clean.

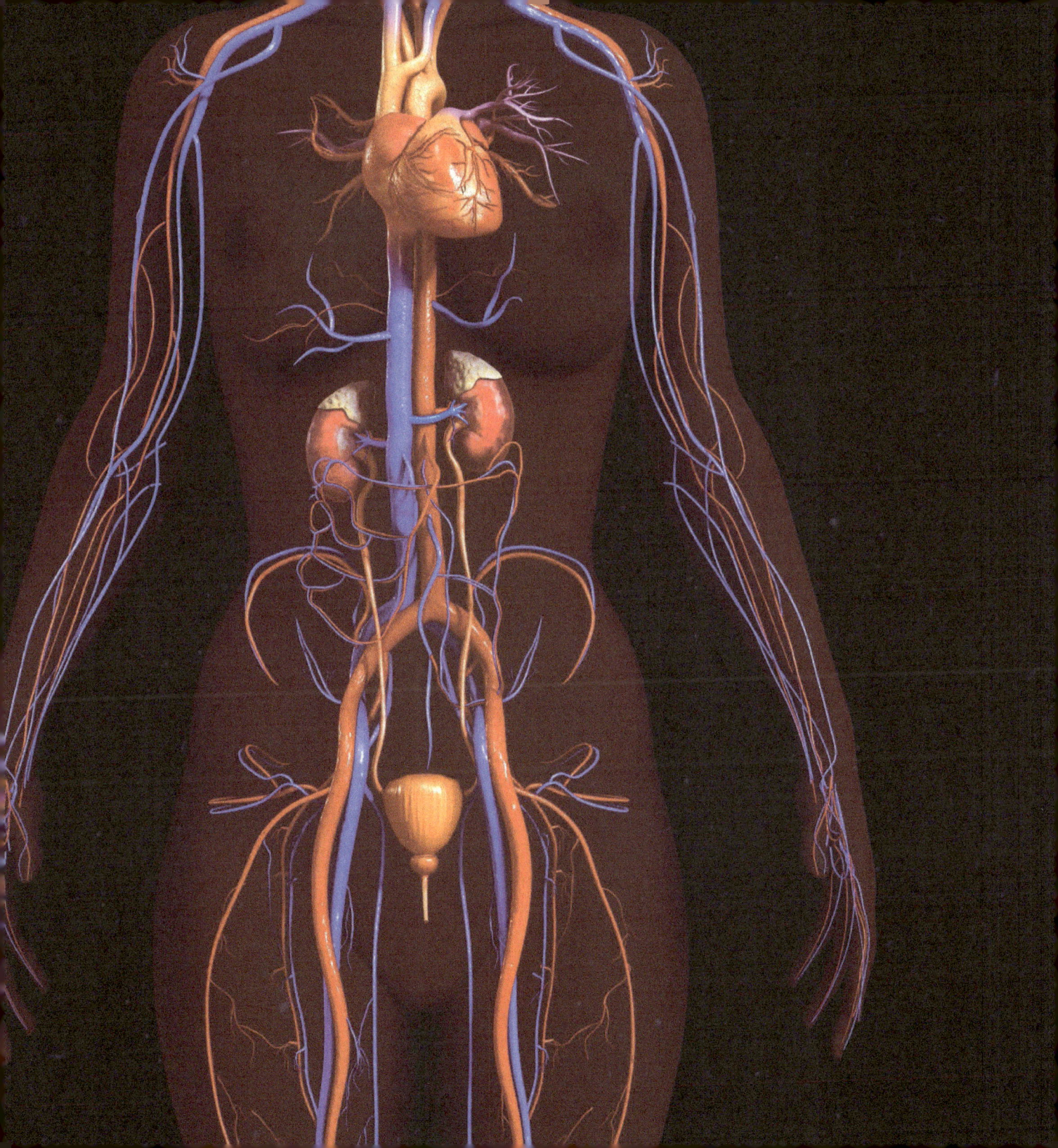

The heart, blood and blood vessels are the main parts of the circulatory system.

Heart – In an average life span, the heart beats three billion times. Each beat is to keep the blood flowing through the body.

IMMUNE SYSTEM

The Immune System protects the body by fighting harmful substances and diseases. An organ in the immune system is the skin.

Skin – It is considered as one of the most important and the largest part of our body. It is the protective covering of our body. It is made up of three layers and the epidermis is the outer layer.

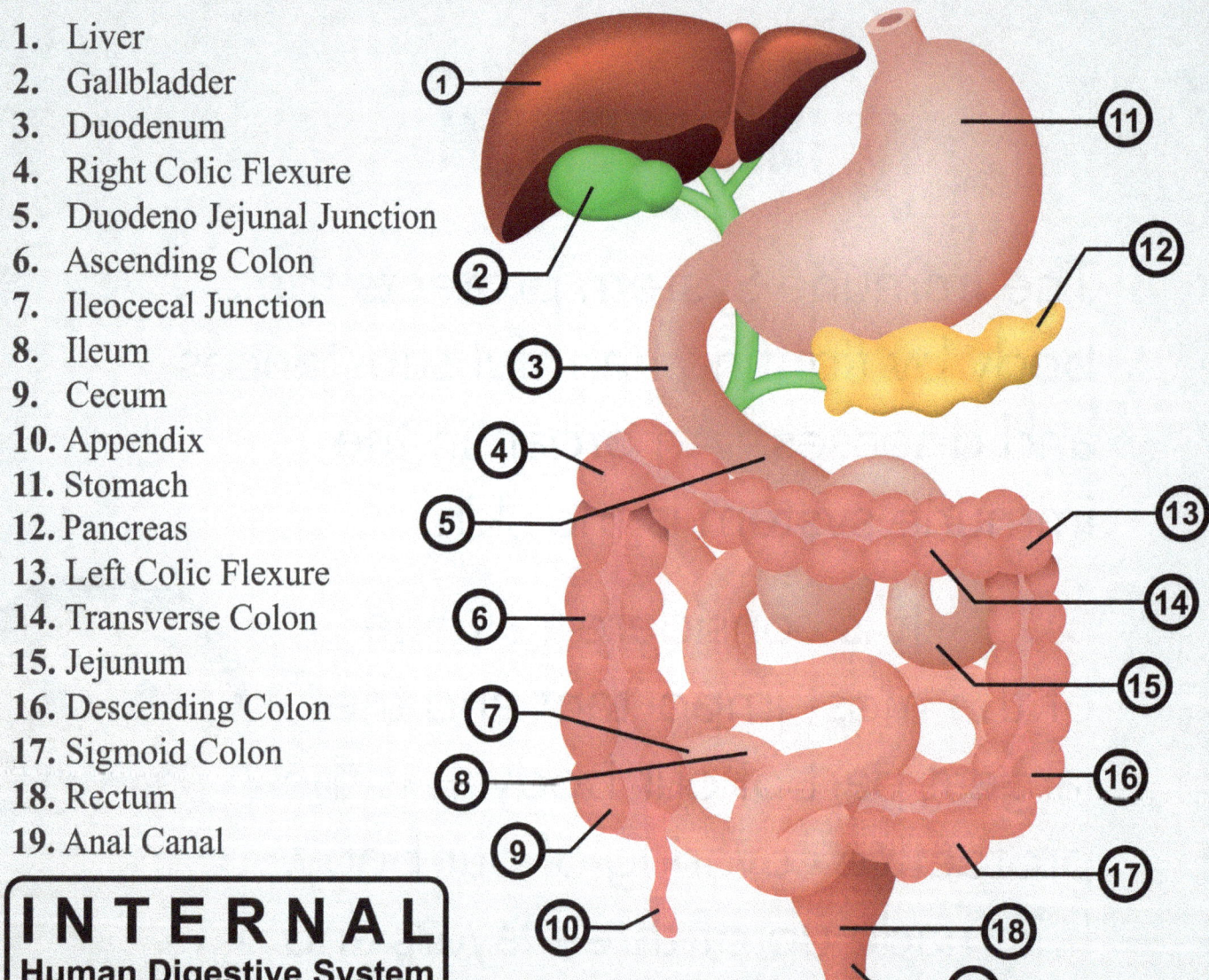

DIGESTIVE SYSTEM

Teeth – When we eat, we use our teeth to chew the food and the digestive enzymes in the saliva help process the food. It is responsible for breaking down food into tiny particles. It is done through the mouth, esophagus, stomach and intestines. The food is passed through them so the body can keep and use the nutrients it needs.

SKELETAL SYSTEM

It protects the major organs of the body and allows them to move.

Bones - They give structure and strength to our body. The cartilage, joints and ligaments connect the bones. There are 200 bones in our body.

Human Skeleton

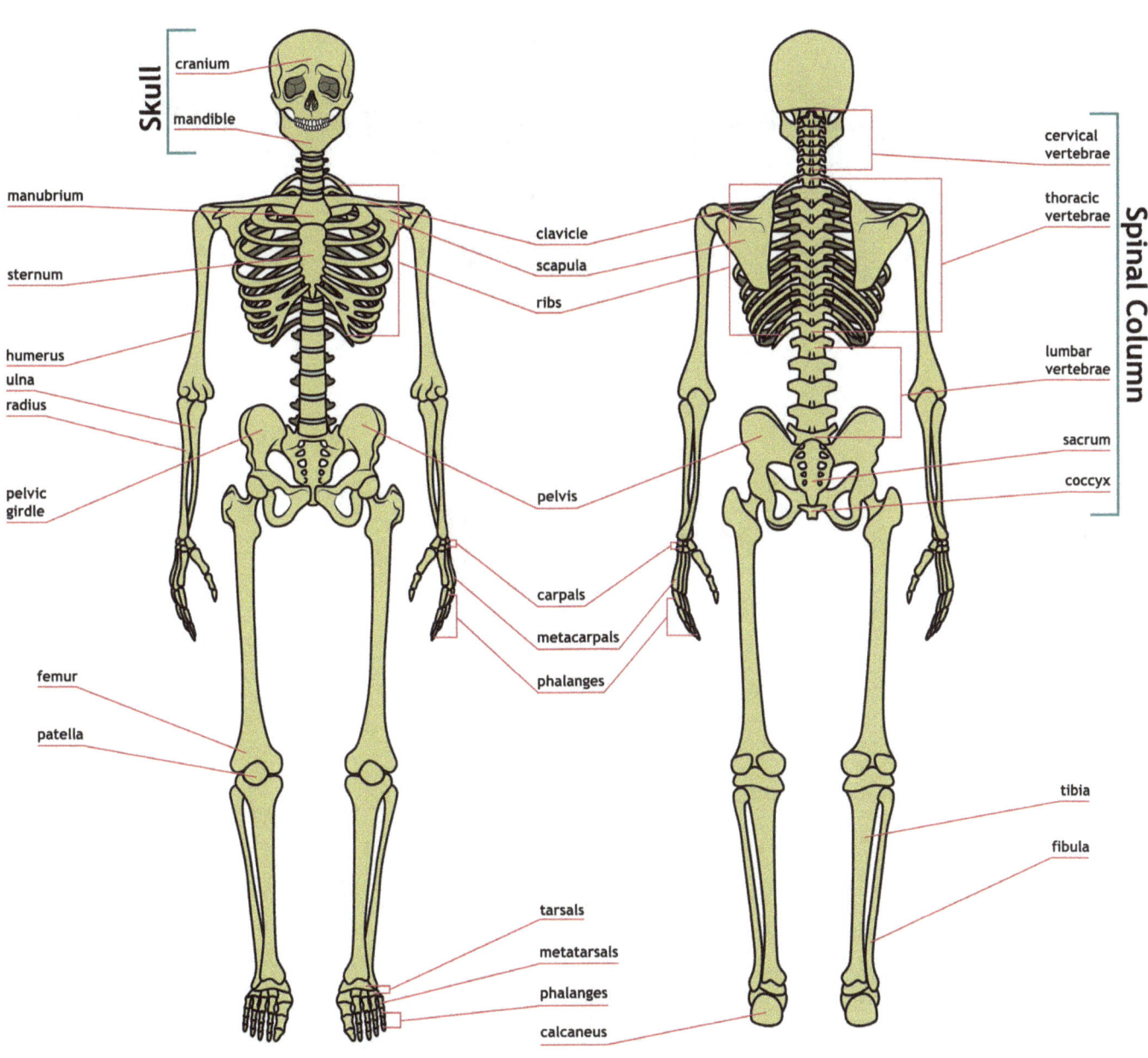

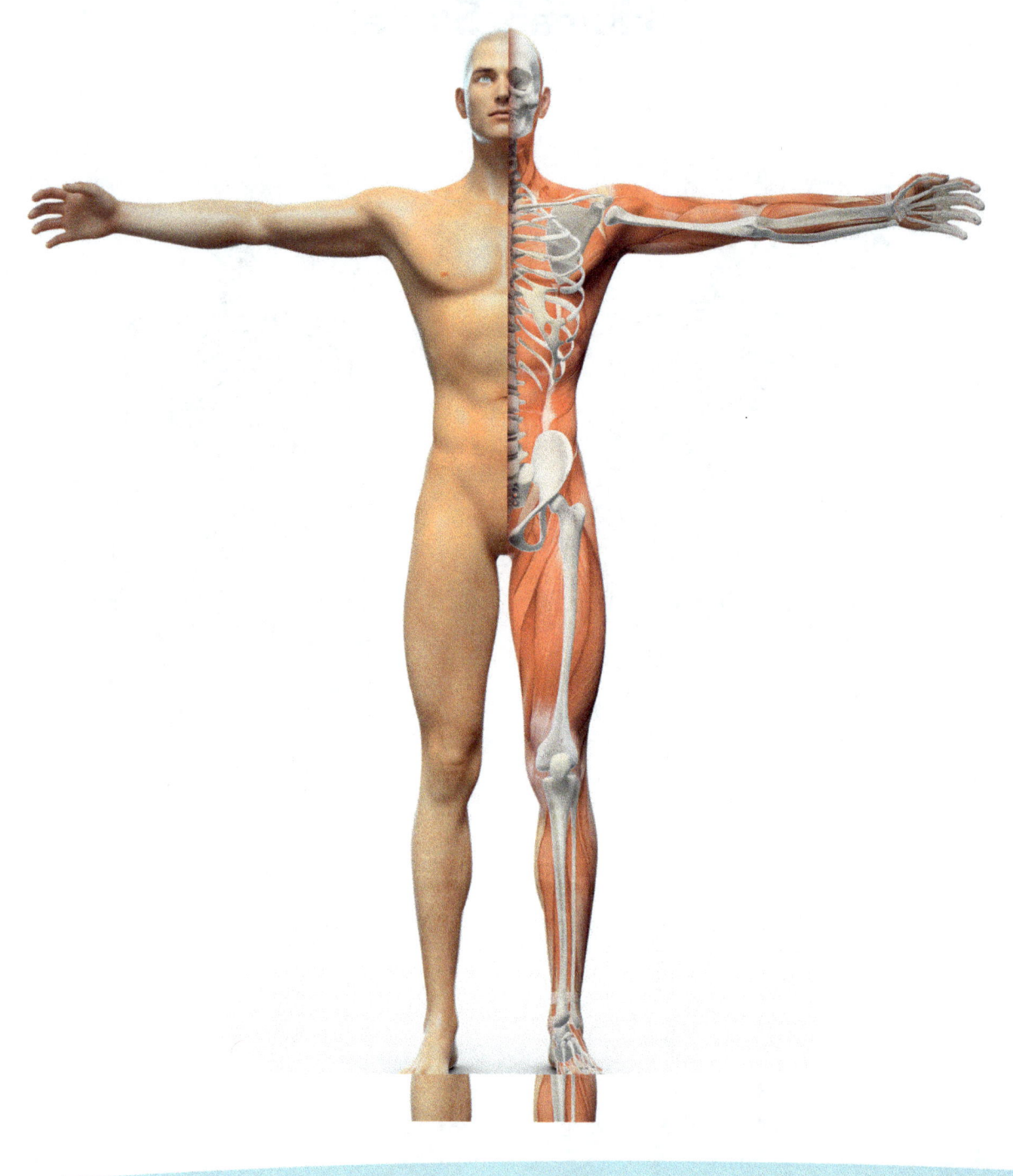

MUSCULAR SYSTEM

It helps the body move. Involuntary muscles are muscles that can't be controlled while voluntary muscles are muscles that can be controlled.

Muscles - They make us move. Our body is composed of more than 600 muscles.

RESPIRATORY SYSTEM

It is responsible of bringing oxygen into the human body.

Lungs - They help us breathe by taking oxygen from the air and releasing carbon dioxide.

Nose - It is used to inhale air and to identify the different smells around us. It is one of the main organs of the respiratory system.

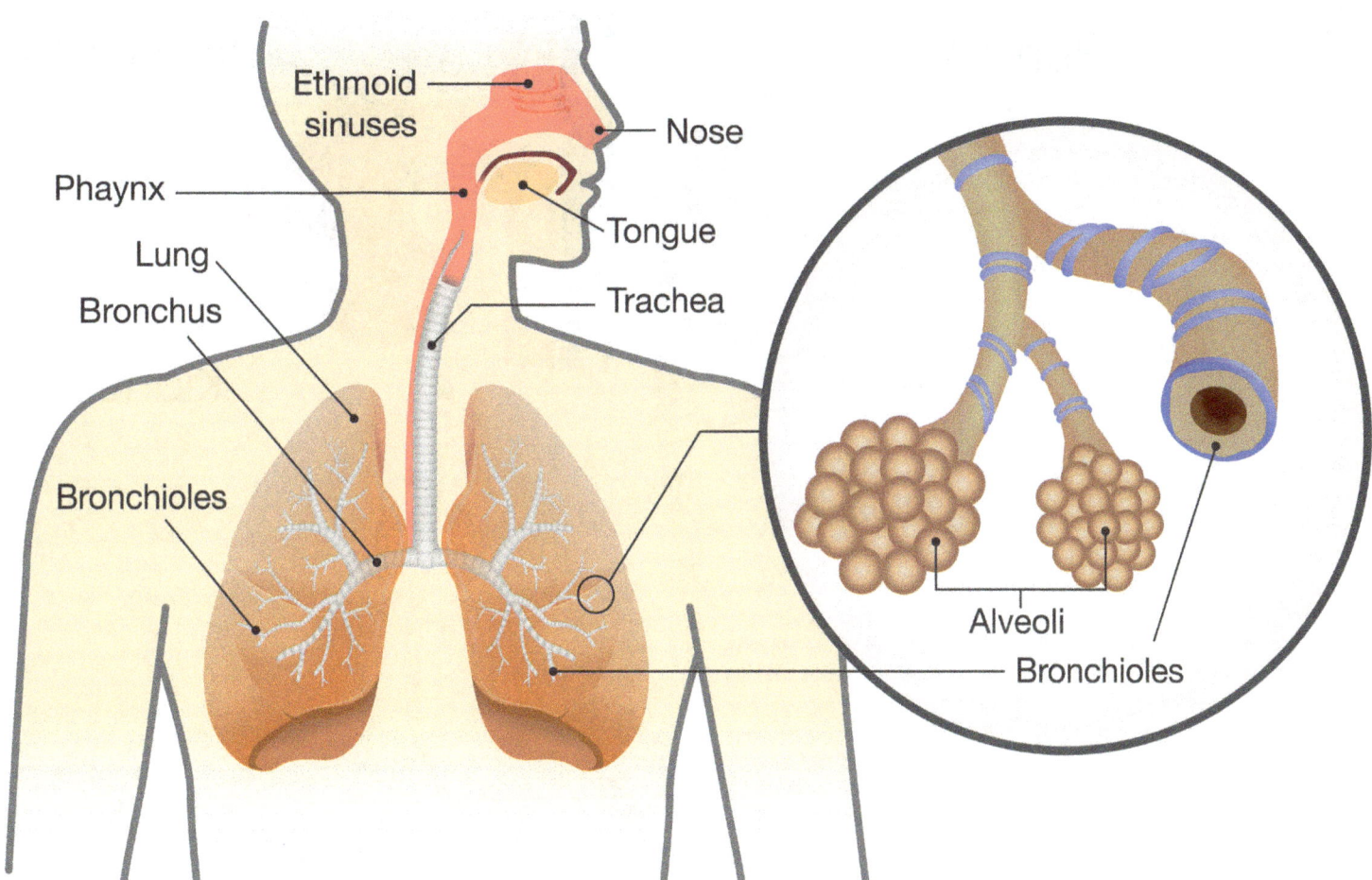

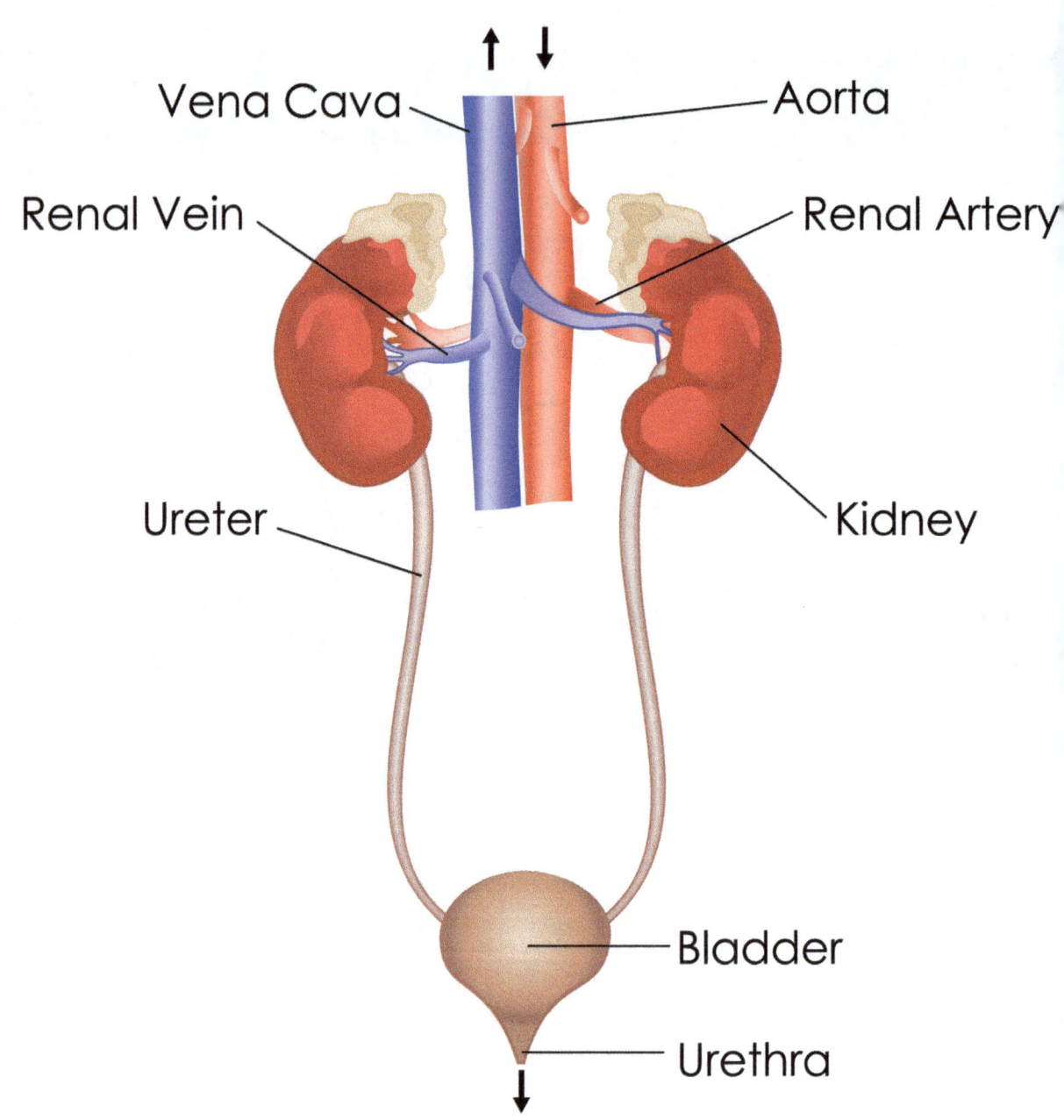

EXCRETORY SYSTEM

It is responsible for expelling toxins and is very important in keeping the body clean. The kidney, liver and skin are the most important organs in the excretory system.

Liver - It filters wastes and removes them from the body.

Kidneys - They remove excess salt out of the body.

OTHER IMPORTANT BODY PARTS:

Eyes - Our eyes are an important part of the body. They allow us to see the things around us. They are composed of three layers namely the vascular, nervous and the fibrous layer.

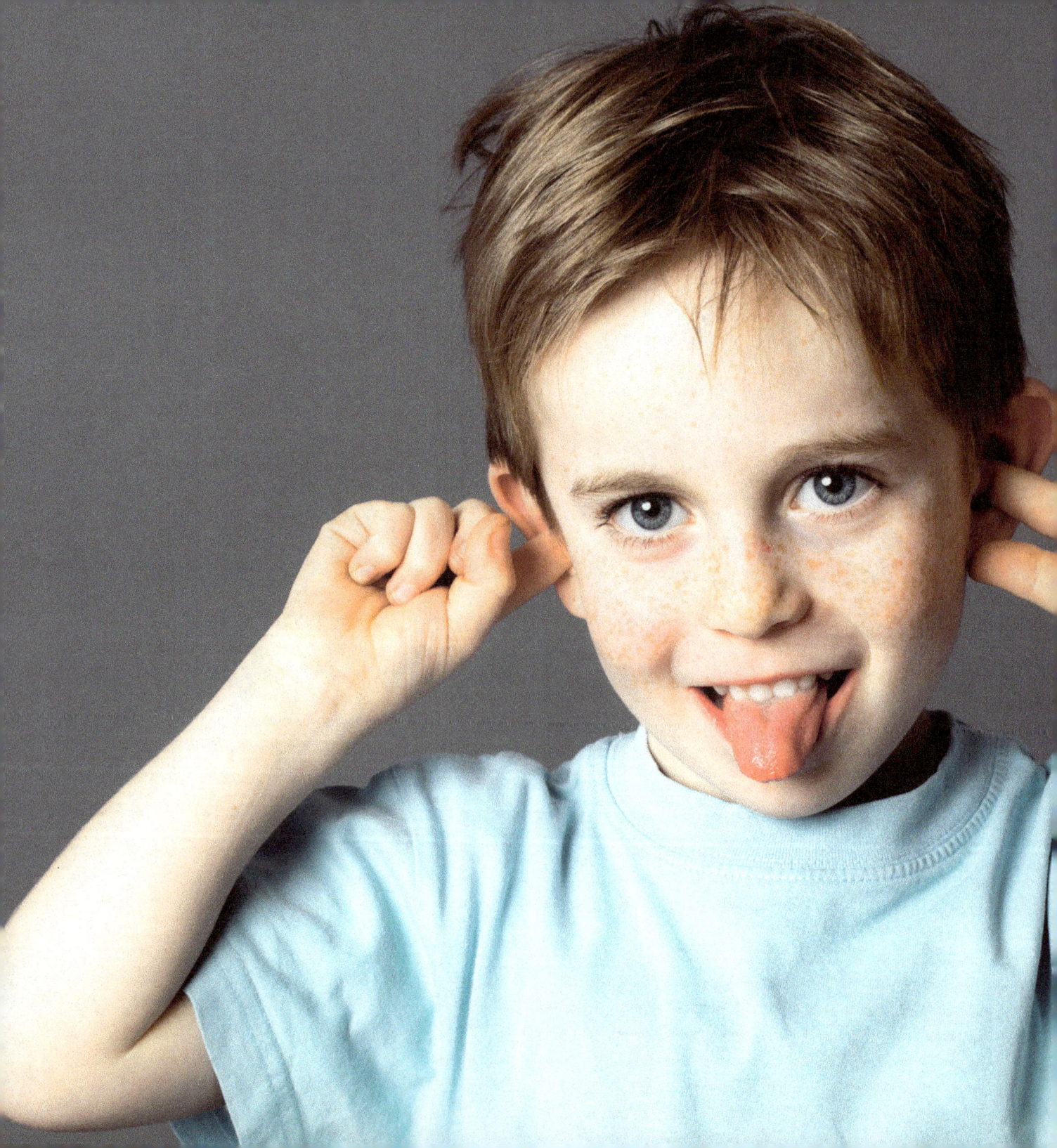

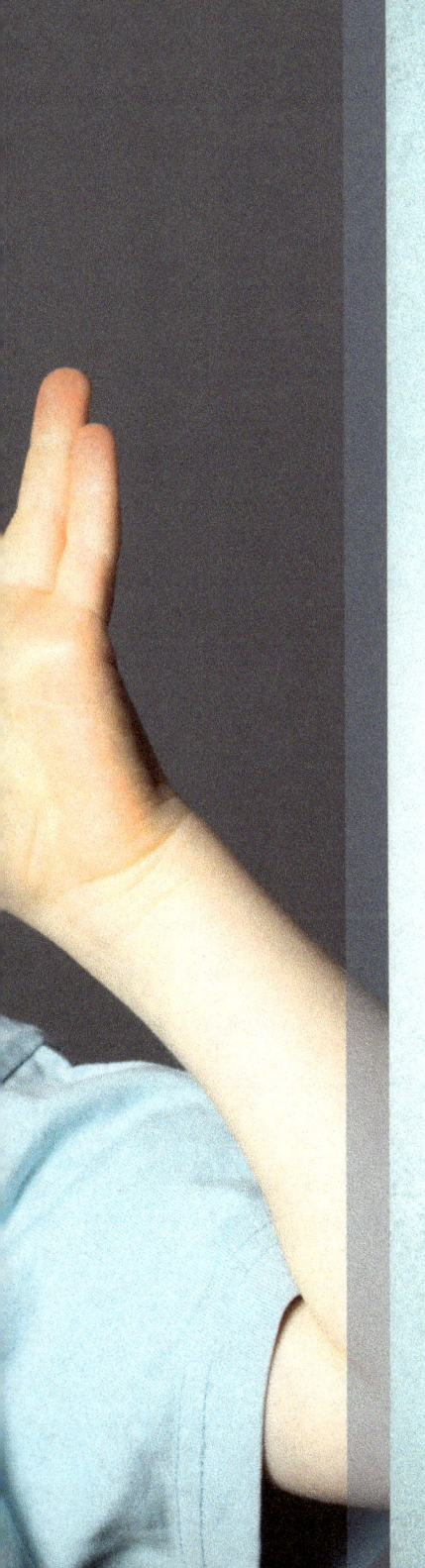

Tongue - It is covered with taste buds and helps us tastes food.

Ears- They allow us to hear sounds and to keep the body's balance. Our ears can be divided into three sections called the outer ear, the middle ear and the inner ear.

Neck- It connects the head to the rest of the body. The base of the skull is attached to the shoulders and the spine through the neck. Aside from these, the neck is also responsible for the movement of the head.

Shoulders - They are load-bearing joints. They connect the arms to the rest of the body.

Legs and Arms - They make the human body mobile. The arms are limbs that allow us to perform complex actions while the legs carry our weight and help us move to different places.

Hair – It is found all over the body except on the palms of the hands, lips and soles. Hair is made up of keratin, which is a special kind of protein.

Learning about the human body is fun!

Now pass the knowledge on!

www.ingramcontent.com/pod-product-compliance
Lightning Source LLC
LaVergne TN
LVHW061321060426
835507LV00019B/2254